HAMMERING FOR FREEDOM

THE WILLIAM LEWIS STORY

Rita Lorraine Hubbard

illustrated by John Holyfield

Lee & Low Books Inc.
New York

LEE & LOW BOOKS Inc., 95 Madison Avenue, New York, NY 10016
leeandlow.com
Edited by Jessica V. Echeverria
Designed by Christy Hale
Book production by The Kids at Our House
The text is set in ITC Century
The illustrations are rendered in acrylic
Manufactured in China by Toppan
10 9 8 7 6 5 4 3 2 1
First Edition

Library of Congress Cataloging-in-Publication Data
Names: Hubbard, Rita L., author. | Holyfield, John, illustrator.
Title: Hammering for freedom: the William Lewis story
by Rita Lorraine Hubbard; illustrations by John Holyfield.
Description: First edition. | New York: Lee & Low Books, 2018.
Identifiers: LCCN 2017053440 | ISBN 9781600609695 (hardcover: alk. paper)
Subjects: LCSH: Lewis, William, 1810-1896—Juvenile literature. |
Freedmen—Tennessee—Chattanooga—Biography—Juvenile literature. |
Blacksmiths—Tennessee—Chattanooga—Biography—Juvenile literature. |
African Americans—Tennessee—Chattanooga—Biography—Juvenile literature.
African Americans—Tennessee—Chattanooga—History—Juvenile literature.
Chattanooga (Tenn.)—Biography—Juvenile literature. | Chattanooga
(Tenn.)—History—Juvenile literature.
Classification: LCC F444.C453 L494 2018 | DDC 682.092 [B]—dc23
LC record available at https://lccn.loc.gov/2017053440

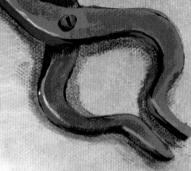

To my family, thanks for the memories —R.L.H.

To Scott, thank you for the love and inspiration —J.H.

One starry night in 1810, William "Bill" Lewis was born on a plantation in Winchester, Tennessee. Bill and his family were enslaved and worked long, grueling days in Colonel Lewis's fields. Each evening, after the sun had disappeared and had taken all the colors with it, Bill and his mother, aunt, brothers, and sister returned to their little cabin, exhausted.

Bill watched his mother, Jenny, droop like a wilted flower and lower herself onto a rickety stool to rest. He stood close to comfort her, and wished he could do more.

As soon as Bill was old enough to grip a hammer, Colonel Lewis decided that the young boy should be a blacksmith. Bill put away tools, swept ashes, and hauled coal and water. Later he learned to fit hinge joints together, make and repair tools, and work with fire.

Bill had not asked to become a blacksmith, but he was very good at it. People paid Colonel Lewis to have Bill fix their broken things. He earned so much money fixing old tools and creating new ones that Colonel Lewis let Bill keep a little money for himself.

As Bill's stack of coins grew, so did his hopes and dreams. Each coin he saved brought him closer to purchasing his freedom. Once he was free, he could spend his money on whatever he wanted. And what he wanted was to free his family.

Year after year, Bill hammered steel, forged tools, and saved the few coins he was allowed to keep. When he was in his twenties, he married a kind woman named Jane, and a few years later, they had a son named Eldridge. As Bill settled his plump, squirming baby in the crook of his arm, he felt a new weight of responsibility. He would have to work longer and harder if he was going to change his family's circumstances.

Bill had been doing more than saving all these years: He had also been planning. He knew slave owners often rented out enslaved men and women to make extra money, so Bill decided to ask Colonel Lewis to let him rent *himself*. If the colonel agreed, Bill's time would be his own to work day and night—as many hours as he could stand—until he saved enough to free not only Jane and Eldridge, but also his mother, aunt, brothers, and sister.

Colonel Lewis thought carefully about this proposal. He had one condition. "Pay me three hundred fifty dollars a year to rent your freedom," he said, "and you can keep whatever else you earn."

Bill agreed. At twenty-seven years old, he set his daring plan in motion.

After he paid Colonel Lewis the rent from his savings, Bill still had enough money to open his own blacksmith shop. He chose the perfect location: a bustling little city called Chattanooga that needed a handy blacksmith. Bill packed his tools and his dreams, and with a heavy heart, left Jane, baby Eldridge, and his other family members behind.

In 1837, when he opened his shop on Market Street, Bill made history as the first African American blacksmith in the city.

Ding! Ching!

Wearing a thick leather apron to protect against flying sparks, Bill went to work on his first job: the bell and clapper for the little log building sitting right in the middle of town. When the bell sounded, Chattanoogans would know a town meeting was about to begin.

Every morning, while the sky was still purple and blue, Bill stretched his muscles and gripped a hammer.

Clang! Clang!

All through the day, his hammer sang its song. The white-hot iron spat liquid fire as Bill forged and shaped scythes, mallets, and other instruments, which he sold for fifty cents or one dollar to his many customers.

Ding! Ching!

When other shops closed for the day, Bill kept working. He didn't stop until the burnt-orange sky faded to patchy black.

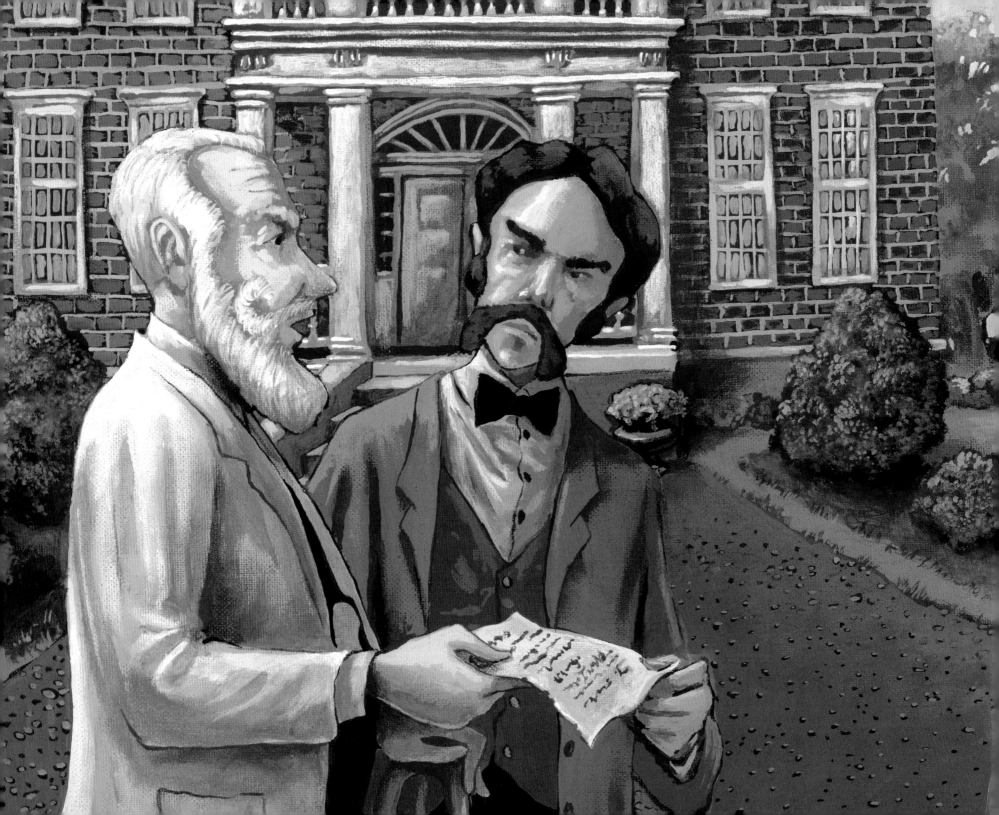

Bill was ready for the next step in his plan: buying Jane's freedom. Once Jane was free, any future children she and Bill had would also be free.

Bill traveled back to the Lewis plantation with a white escort who would handle the transaction with the colonel.

Bill and Jane held their breath as the escort handed over the payment.

"This makes one thousand dollars," said Colonel Lewis. "Jane is free."

The expressions on Bill's and Jane's faces did not change in front of the colonel. But when they were safely home in Chattanooga, they celebrated Jane's freedom.

Bill got right back to work.

Ding! Ching!

Bill's workday consisted of more than just fixing old tools. He also created special nails that could be used to secure horseshoes. He sold these for a few pennies each. When he built new wagons that farmers used to haul vegetables, hay, and family members, Bill charged as much as five dollars and fifty cents per job. People everywhere depended on Bill's calloused, talented hands.

After many bone-weary years, Bill returned to Winchester.

"One thousand dollars," Colonel Lewis announced. Then he placed some papers in Bill's hands.

Bill had never learned to read, but he knew what those papers meant.

"Free," he whispered. "I'm free."

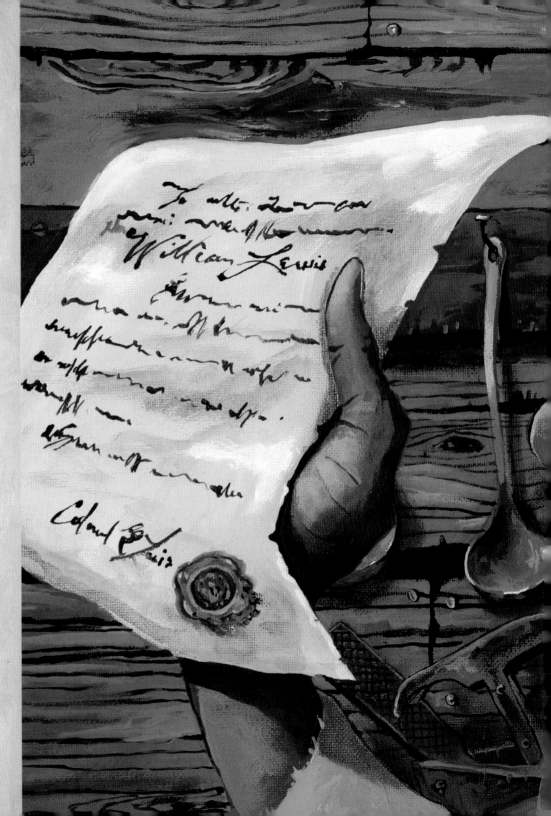

Still, there was no time to waste. *Eldridge is still enslaved*, Bill thought. He needed to save his money all over again to buy his son's freedom.

Clang! Clang!

Hammer and steel rang out as Bill forged every kind of ax, kitchen tool, and utensil imaginable. Customers came from far and wide to buy what Bill made.

Bill returned to Winchester and paid Colonel Lewis four hundred dollars. Then, with a song in his heart, he took Eldridge home to Chattanooga.

Ding! Ching! Clang!

Eldridge proudly watched his father plunge the sizzling tools deep in the water trough. As he grew, Eldridge arranged the new tools on the wall and helped customers in the shop.

Busy as he was, Bill always had time to be a good neighbor. He chatted with customers about the latest news and hired men who needed jobs. He also worshipped in the local Methodist church. The church was segregated, but everyone sang together in songs of praise.

Bill's neighbors, his customers, and the members of the congregation grew to love him as an important member of the community.

In 1851, Bill paid the colonel three hundred dollars, the total asking price for his elderly mother and aunt.

His mother, Jenny, and his aunt hurried toward him with open arms. Then Jenny laid her head on Bill's shoulder. "Hallelujah!" she whispered.

They were finally free.

Bill wanted to shout with joy, but he noticed his siblings' faces. His sister was wiping away tears. His brothers waved slowly and hung their heads.

Bill clenched his jaws with determination. He would simply have to work harder to buy their freedom too.

Ding! Ching!

Bill slung his hammer with such force that his face was drenched with sweat and his chest felt as if it might explode. Somehow he kept working. Dozens of bluish-purple sunrises and burnt-orange sunsets passed before he returned to Winchester with two thousand dollars to buy freedom for his two brothers.

When Bill was nearly fifty, he and Jane realized they needed a bigger house for their ten children and extended family. Bill chose a two-story home with lots of bedrooms and a big front porch that the family could enjoy. People were stunned when Bill paid two thousand dollars in cash for the house. Most white men could not pay that much money for a home in those days.

Bill and his family settled in and planted a big vegetable garden. The house was more crowded than ever, but someone was missing. Bill's sister was still enslaved.

Bill was much older now than when he first put his plan into action, but he kept on slinging his hammer and saving his money until his sister could finally join them.

Twenty-six years after Bill's arrival in Chattanooga, his plan was complete. He had worked, sweated, and prayed. Now he finally had his loving family around him, just like when he was a boy.

Only now they were all free.

AFTERWORD

William "Bill" Lewis went by many names. As a child, he was known as "Little William, son of Jenny." As an adult, he was called Bill, or sometimes Uncle Bill, by white patrons. No one knows his age for sure; some documents say he was born in 1810 and some say 1815.

William's biological father was Colonel James Lewis, a veteran of the Revolutionary War who was granted thousands of acres of land for his service. The US Census of 1840 states that Colonel James Lewis and members of his extended family owned thirty slaves—sixteen males and fourteen females.

Bill married Jane sometime in the 1830s. Their son Eldridge was born between 1835 and 1838. As an enslaved man, Bill was not permitted to travel alone or handle his own financial transactions, which is why he needed a white escort to pay Colonel Lewis for Jane's freedom. In freeing Jane first, their children (after Eldridge) would be born free. It is known that their next child, Marion Isabel, was born free in 1842 or 1843.

Bill and Jane had ten children: Eldridge, Marion Isabel, Hugh, Mary, Jennie, Willianna, Elizabeth, James, Hickman, and Sueda. Although Bill and Jane never learned to read or write, they still managed to give their children a good education. Marion Isabel graduated from Oberlin College and married attorney John H. Cook, who later became dean of Howard University Law School. Sueda was a teacher in Washington, DC, and Hickman served as a mail carrier. Eldridge worked in Bill's blacksmith shop for many years. James also worked in the blacksmith shop, but later moved on to other jobs. Hugh enlisted in the United States Colored Troops in 1864 to fight in the Civil War, but he died of a fever in Wilmington, North Carolina, the following year.

Bill earned a considerable fortune as a free blacksmith. According to a 1993 article in the *Chattanooga News-Free Press*, Bill paid $2,000 cash to Chattanooga pioneer Bill Crutchfield for the Market Street location where he would operate his blacksmith shop. His first job was working on the bell that summoned citizens to community gatherings in Chattanooga.

Over the years, Bill's assets increased from $1,500 in 1850 to $7,000 in 1860—the equivalent of $200,000 today. During the Civil War, Bill was asked to use his blacksmithing skills to shackle Andrews' Raiders, a group of Union spies. On April 12, 1862, the Raiders stole a Confederate train and drove it through northern Georgia, destroying railroad tracks and cutting telegraph wires along the way. They were captured and eventually imprisoned in Chattanooga. By this time, Bill had worked so hard he had injured himself, and he could only supervise while one of his sons created leg irons for the Raiders. It is not known how Bill felt about shackling them, but he did ask permission to send them lettuce from his family garden as a gesture of friendship.

Convinced that the South would lose the Civil War, Bill invested some of his money in tobacco, which he stored until it was worth much more than he had paid. He eventually sold it for a handsome profit. When Union soldiers took over Chattanooga during the war, Bill's blacksmith shop was seized, and like so many other wealthy Southerners, the bulk of his fortune quickly disappeared. By 1870, his net worth had dwindled to $300 and he and Jane filed for a government pension. Still, their good reputation earned them a prized invitation to attend the wedding of Booker T. Washington in 1892. It is unclear whether they were able to attend.

Bill died on September 2, 1896, when he was about eighty-six years old. His obituary said he left behind "a host of friends, both white and colored, and always bore an excellent record for thrift, honesty and sobriety."

A host of friends was not all he left behind. A building plaque in his memory is located in the heart of downtown Chattanooga on the corner of Market and Seventh Streets. There is a historical marker erected in his honor on Market Street too. Bill also left behind a devoted wife, nine children, and many descendants that would never have existed if he had not forged his daring plan to free his family.